A CLOSER LOOK BOOK
© The Archon Press Ltd
1976

Designed by David Cook and
Associates and produced by
The Archon Press Ltd
28 Percy Street
London W1P 9FF

Dr L. B. Halstead, Ph.D., D.Sc.,
is Reader in Geology and
Zoology at the University of
Reading, and Research Fellow
at the Royal Dental Hospital,
London.

First published in
Great Britain 1976 by
Hamish Hamilton
Children's Books Ltd
90 Great Russell Street
London WC1B 3PT

0 241 89389 5

Printed in Great Britain by
W. S. Cowell Ltd
Butter Market, Ipswich

A closer LOOK at

PREHISTORIC MAMMALS

Beverly Halstead

Illustrated by

P. Barrett, G. Caselli, R. Orr

Hamish Hamilton · London

The story in the rocks

It is difficult to imagine a time when there were neither human beings nor animals on the earth at all, but life as we know it today has not always been the same. It was not suddenly created, as people once believed, but is the result of gradual changes that have taken millions of years. Only in the last hundred years has this theory of evolution come to be accepted as scientific fact.

Just as we know the history of our country from historical documents, so we know the history of our life on earth from the preserved 'documents' of the past geological ages. The 'book' that tells us most is the earth itself. The 'pages' are the layers, or strata, of rock, and the 'words' are the fossilised remains of past life, fossils in the form of bones, teeth and shells. Sometimes 'sentences' are incomplete or missing altogether, and then an expert has to interpret or translate the 'words'.

By studying the preserved remains of past ages, we can trace each stage of evolution. Fossils found at different rock levels reveal that the first vertebrates, or animals with backbones, developed about 500 million years ago. They lived first in the sea, but about 100 million years later, the fish began to invade freshwater lakes and rivers. About 55 million years after that, the first amphibians – animals that can live either on land or in water – ventured on to land, and 300 million years ago the first reptiles evolved. These laid eggs in shells.

But the real conquest of the land came 280 million years ago, when the ancestors of the mammals began to spread across the continents. After dominating the earth for 70 million years, they eventually gave way to the true mammals. The development of these true mammals coincided with that of the dinosaurs, the dominant land animals for the next 140 million years. When the dinosaurs died out, 64 million years ago, the age of the mammals at last dawned. It culminated three million years ago with the arrival of mankind.

Life on earth

Our earth is about 4,500 million years old, and the first evidence of life dates from 3,000 million years ago. Since that time, life has developed into many varied forms. There are today, for example, more than 300,000 species, or types, of plant, ranging from mosses and fungi to giant tropical trees. There are more than one million species of animal, and they include forms as varied as grasshoppers, sharks, snakes, eagles and kangaroos. And there is man himself. None of these plants or animals would now exist had they been unable to adapt to changing conditions. The diagram shows the names given to the geological periods of the earth's history, measured in millions of years.

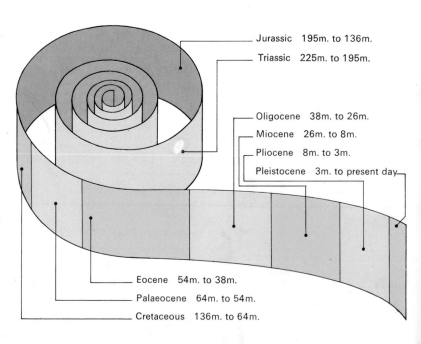

Jurassic 195m. to 136m.
Triassic 225m. to 195m.
Oligocene 38m. to 26m.
Miocene 26m. to 8m.
Pliocene 8m. to 3m.
Pleistocene 3m. to present day
Eocene 54m. to 38m.
Palaeocene 64m. to 54m.
Cretaceous 136m. to 64m.

Fossilisation

This *Arsinotherium* lived and died over 30 million years ago. Slowly, the sands of a river estuary covered its skeleton and, in time, hardened around it into sedimentary rock. Protected in this way, the bones of *Arsinotherium* did not disintegrate; instead, together with other forms of plant and animal life, they were preserved as fossils.

Millions of years later, other sedimentary rocks covered the layers in which *Arsinotherium* was buried. At first, because overlying water brought in sand and mud, the sedimentary strata, or layers, were flat, but earth movements later uplifted and distorted them. This is why it is possible to find sedimentary layers far above sea level where they originated.

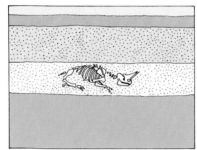
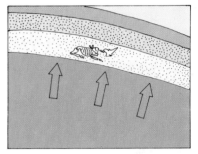

Sedimentary strata are soft rocks, unable to withstand erosion from water and other natural forces. These forces combine to cut gorges through the strata; when this happens, they expose fossils like that of *Arsinotherium*. A palaeontologist, a person who studies fossils, will take infinite time and trouble to remove the fossil bones from the rock.

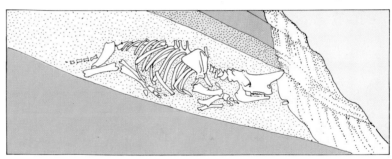

Dating fossils

Fossils are dated by the age of the surrounding rock. The oldest layers of sediment are found at the bottom, the youngest at the top. The relative ages of rocks belonging to the age of mammals are deduced largely by the proportion of modern-type sea shells found within them. Rocks from the Palaeocene and Eocene periods have very few shells; those from the Oligocene and Miocene have more, and most are found in the more recent Pliocene and Pleistocene rocks. Nearly all the shells of the Pleistocene are modern. Using these clues, it is possible to date fossils in terms of geological periods. More precise dating is achieved by examining the radio-active minerals in the rock.

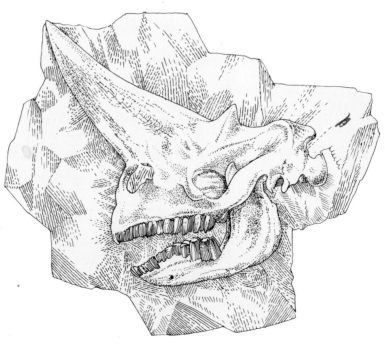

What are mammals?

The fundamental feature of all mammals is that the young are suckled at the mother's breast (the word mammal is based on the Latin word for breasts, 'mammae'). This method of feeding means that they are completely dependent on the mother during the early stages of development and cannot fend for themselves, as reptiles do. Young mammals depend upon their parents for longer than any other animals, and it is during this period that they learn their skills for survival throughout life.

To allow the young mammal to suck at the mother's breast and breathe at the same time, a bony secondary palate separates the air and food passages. This enables them to keep food in their mouths and to chew or grind it while breathing.

All mammals are warm-blooded and maintain a constant internal temperature. They do so by burning up their food to produce energy at a fast rate, but they can only do this if the supply of oxygen to the lungs is constant, even during feeding. Once again, the secondary palate is vital. Temperature is maintained also by insulating hair or fur, and by sweating, which cools down the body.

Mammals have different kinds of teeth. Since teeth are not needed for drinking milk, the animals rarely have any at all at birth. A set of 'milk' teeth develop later, but they are shed and replaced by incisors for plucking or pulling food, canines for stabbing or tearing, and premolars and molars for grinding or chewing.

Another remarkable feature of the mammals, not shared by other animals, is their middle ear. The three bones – the hammer, anvil and stirrup – act as a sound amplification system so that any sound becomes louder as it travels from bone to bone.

Perhaps the most significant feature of the mammals, however, is their intelligence. It is to this characteristic above all others that mammals owe their present-day success.

The world of vertebrates

All mammals are vertebrates. Whereas insects and shellfish have no external skeletons, and worms have no skeletons at all, vertebrates have a backbone and an internal skeleton. Because of its flexibility, an internal skeleton makes the animal more adaptable for living, and vertebrates range in size from the 27 metre long blue whale, which can weigh as much as 150 tonnes, to the 65 millimetre long pygmy shrew.

Vertebrates successfully inhabit land, sea and air; they include fish, amphibia, reptiles, mammals and birds, and they evolved in that sequence. The higher vertebrates – mammals and birds – unlike the others, are warm-blooded.

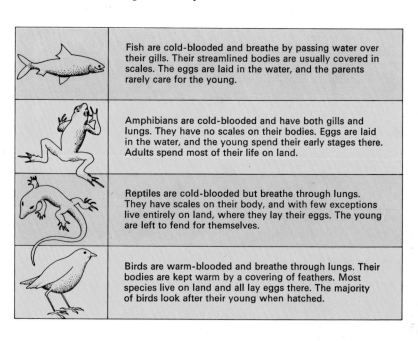

Fish are cold-blooded and breathe by passing water over their gills. Their streamlined bodies are usually covered in scales. The eggs are laid in the water, and the parents rarely care for the young.

Amphibians are cold-blooded and have both gills and lungs. They have no scales on their bodies. Eggs are laid in the water, and the young spend their early stages there. Adults spend most of their life on land.

Reptiles are cold-blooded but breathe through lungs. They have scales on their body, and with few exceptions live entirely on land, where they lay their eggs. The young are left to fend for themselves.

Birds are warm-blooded and breathe through lungs. Their bodies are kept warm by a covering of feathers. Most species live on land and all lay eggs there. The majority of birds look after their young when hatched.

Reproduction

Mammals have three different ways of giving birth. The rarest is that of the monotremes, the most successful that of the placental mammals.

Monotremes

The spiny ant-eater of Australia is a monotreme. It lays an egg and transfers it to a pouch where there are glands on which the infant will suckle.

Marsupial mammals

Marsupials also have pouches but instead of laying eggs, they give birth to a tiny embryo. The infant makes its way into the pouch where there are nipples.

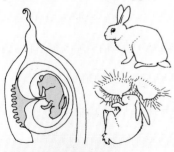

Placental mammals

The young placental mammal develops inside the mother for a longer period. After birth, the mother suckles the infant at her breast.

A typical mammal

The mouse possesses all the features that have made mammals so successful. The brain is complex, and a set of bones in the inner ear transmit and amplify sound. A secondary palate separates the air and food passages, which allows the animal to eat and breathe at the same time. A thick layer of fur keeps it warm, and the young are born live and suckle at the mother's breast.

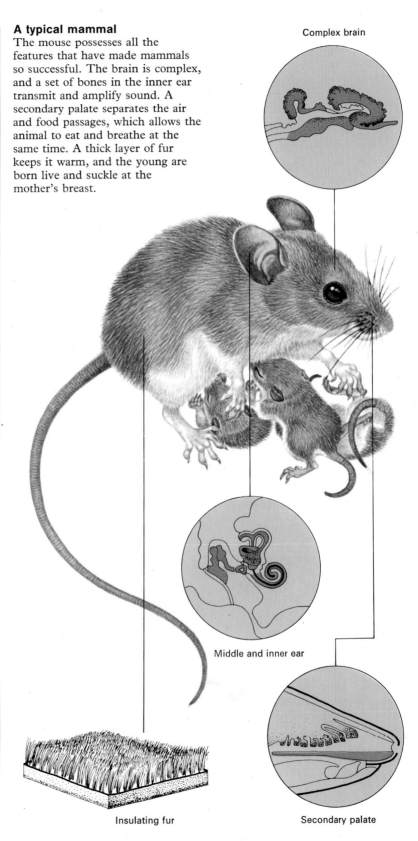

Complex brain

Middle and inner ear

Insulating fur

Secondary palate

The beginnings

The first reptiles which lived in the swamps and coal forests that covered northern Europe and North America, 300 million years ago, were the ancestors of the mammals. When the swamps dried up, these paramammals spread across the dry land. At first they were fish-eaters – their numerous, sharp-pointed teeth were merely fish traps – but gradually they developed stronger jaws and long stabbing teeth for holding and killing other prey. Some became plant-eaters, or herbivores; others became flesh-eaters, or carnivores. Originally they had a sprawling posture, with arms and legs sticking out sideways, but as time went by, their limbs straightened and were held below the body. Higher off the ground and with a longer stride, they could now move faster. As well as developing a secondary palate and different kinds of teeth, they evolved necks, and their scales were replaced by insulating hair or fur. These features suggest that the paramammals were warm-blooded and that they suckled their young.

The paramammals were the dominant reptiles on earth for 70 million years. During this long period, their physical structures became more and more mammal-like until eventually, they evolved into true mammals. At this point, however, their development was eclipsed by the advent of the dinosaurs.

Teeth and jaws

Reptile jaws are made of several bones fused together, and contain only one kind of tooth. As reptiles evolved into mammals, some of the bones moved and modified. They became the delicate amplifying bones of the inner ear – the hammer, anvil and stirrup. The mammal jaw is made out of the remaining single bone, and contains different kinds of teeth: molars for grinding, canines for stabbing and incisors for pulling.

Locomotion

Reptiles have a sprawling posture and walk in short strides from the elbow and knee. Mammals, however, have their legs directly beneath them, and move from hip and shoulder.

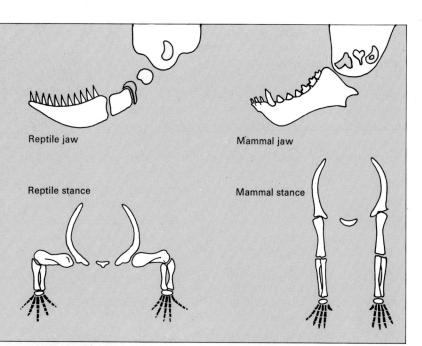

Reptile jaw

Mammal jaw

Reptile stance

Mammal stance

The paramammals

For 70 million years the earth was dominated by mammal-like reptiles such as Cynognathus (1) and Thrimaxodon (2), carnivores; Kannemeyeria (3), a herbivore; and Euparkeria (4), ancestor of the dinosaurs.

The long night

The ancestors of the dinosaurs were small, insect-eating reptiles which originally looked rather like lizards. Gradually they became fast-running, two-footed hunters. It was at the point when some paramammals had become true mammals that the age of the dinosaurs dawned, an age that lasted 140 million years. Although these giant reptiles dominated land, sea and air, it was also, in a modest way, a period of mammalian success; their ability to maintain a constant temperature, their fur, and their rapid rate of reproduction, meant that they could flourish unhindered in the trees and undergrowth during the cool nights while the dinosaurs slept.

There were many groups of tiny mammals, from rat-like plant-eaters to primates, the group to which man belongs; from the ancestors of today's insect-eaters to the clawed condylarths from which carnivores and herbivores descended. Even before the final years of the dinosaur period, the mammals had already evolved the major features which later enabled them to dominate the earth. The area that could support only a few giant dinosaurs could support millions of small mammals. In the end, it was the many small animals that flourished at the expense of the gigantic few.

The age of the dinosaurs

During the 140 million years of the age of the dinosaurs, mammals flourished. Though the giant, cold-blooded dinosaurs, such as Tyrannosaurus (below), dominated the day, they became torpid at night. Then the warm-blooded mammals became active – creatures like Protungulata (below left) and rat-like forms such as Purgatorius (right).

The rise of the mammals

The end of the age of the dinosaurs about 64 million years ago was a sudden and dramatic event, and to this day, the reason for their disappearance remains a mystery. The giants and the smaller flesh-eating dinosaurs all died out, leaving the nocturnal mammals to face a new and freer world. Although lizards, crocodiles, snakes and tortoises were still to be seen, although the skies were filled with birds, this was the beginning of the age of mammals, the start of the Palaeocene period.

No longer did the mammals appear only at night. Now they ventured out in the daytime. Some even came down from the trees, though others (including the primates) did not. Among the new species that developed were the earliest relatives of hares and rabbits. There was, too, a form of flying squirrel; a new group of large herbivores, the pantodonts; and small, weasel-like carnivores which hunted their fellow mammals.

The condylarths continued to flourish as they had done during the reign of the dinosaurs; though they were dominant, the largest of them, *Pantolambda*, was still no bigger than a cow. In spite of the sudden disappearance of the dinosaurs, it seems that the age of mammals got off to only a slow, faltering start.

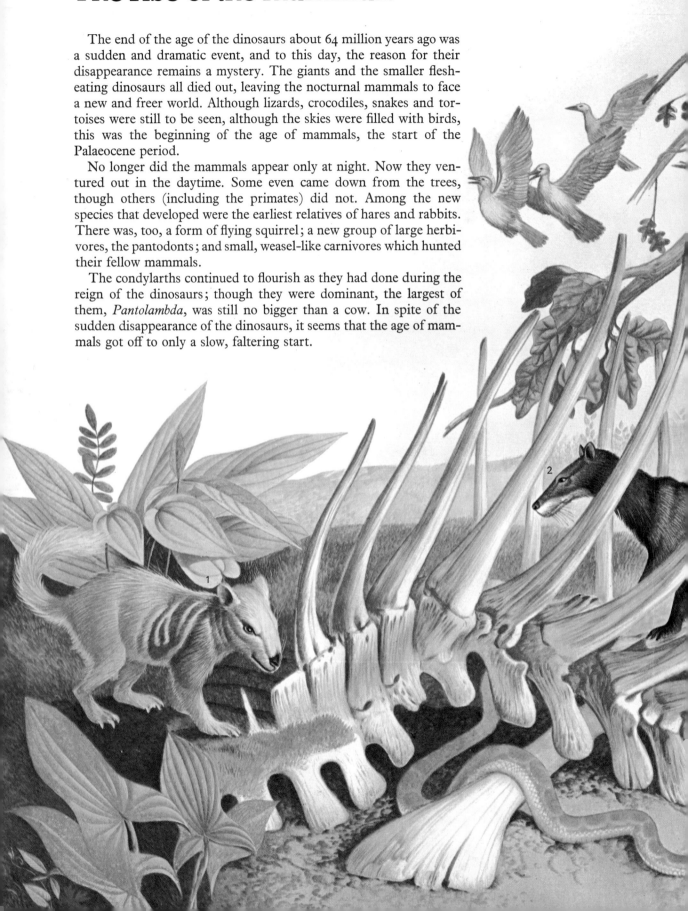

The world to conquer
With the passing of the dinosaurs,
the small nocturnal mammals
ventured out in the daytime.
1. Taeniolabus
2. Protictis
3. Planetetherium
4. Plesiadapis

13

A threat from the birds

Smilodectes

Smilodectes, an ancestor of monkeys, apes and man, belonged to the primates. During this period, trees remained their natural habitat.

The supremacy of the mammals was finally established during the 16-million-year span of the Eocene period. But to begin with, it was doubtful whether they would survive a serious threat.

Birds evolved very rapidly, and even at this time virtually all modern types of birds were already in existence. This in itself did not affect the mammals, for the majority of birds did not compete directly with them for food. But there was one group that did – a group of large, flightless birds called diatrymas.

Diatrymas were immensely large and powerful carnivores and, for a time, it seemed they might become the dominant land animals. Meanwhile, however, the mammals were becoming more diversified; the existence of a single flesh-eating bird endangered only temporarily their overall advance. *Diatryma* merely filled the niche of flesh-eaters until the mammals were able to cope satisfactorily.

The largest mammal of the Eocene was *Uintatherium*, a rhinoceros-sized herbivore recognisable by the bony horns on its skull and long, dagger-like canine teeth. There was *Coryphodon*, which resembled a hippopotamus; there was the small *Hyracotherium*, the ancestor of the horse; and there were the condylarths which, by this time, had developed hooves and were plant-eaters.

But the most striking developments were to be seen in the archaic carnivores, or creodonts. The wolf-sized mesonychids, for example, learned to run; the oxyaenids had short faces and powerful, clawed limbs; the massively built hyaenodonts seem to have been scavengers; and another group of flesh-eating mammals, the smaller miacids, occupied the role filled today by genets and civets.

Throughout this time, and once the threat from the diatrymas had faded, the most successful mammals were the forest-dwelling herbivores and carnivores. Although the miacids were not particularly dominant, however, one of their features proved critical to their future survival and success: they had better brains than other carnivores.

An Eocene landscape
In the Eocene period some larger mammals like the Uintatherium (1), as large as a present-day rhino, and Coryphodon (2), about the size of a small hippo, developed. The small ancestor of the horse, Hyracotherium, was the prey of both the early carnivore Oxyaena (3), puma sized, and the giant flightless bird Diatryma (4). Diatryma had a head the size of that of a modern horse.

R. ORR

The triumph of the mammals

Aegyptopithecus

Aegyptopithecus, a primate which lived 35 million years ago, is an ancestor of both apes and man. Fossils have been found in Egypt.

Throughout the Oligocene period, which lasted 12 million years and witnessed the transition to the modern world, the mammals were the undisputed masters of the earth. For many of the most successful of the earlier ones, however, it was a period of crisis which ended in their extinction. They were replaced by forms better able to adapt to changing conditions.

The dense forests of the Eocene period began to give way to more open country. Robbed of the protection of the forests, herbivores developed longer legs, for they had to be able to escape from predators at faster speeds. Primitive camels, antelope and horses abounded. As well as improvements in locomotion, teeth also gradually adapted to cope with the spreading grasslands. Some herbivores, however, such as the strangely-horned titanotheres and the huge, hornless *Paraceratherium*, were too large to survive. Their appetites were so great that the changing landscape could no longer provide sufficient food for them.

Other victims of the new grasslands were the ancient carnivores whose traditional prey could now out-run them. Only the scavenging hyaenodonts survived; the rest simply died out.

The Oligocene marks the first point in the natural history of the world when the highest premium was on brain power. The first true dogs and cats evolved; their advantage was neither speed nor power but the intelligence to outwit their enemies. Meanwhile, in Egypt, the primate *Aegyptopithecus* marked the beginning of the line that led to apes and man. Their intelligence, again, was the key to success.

Carnivores

When the archaic carnivores died out, only the scavenging hyaenodonts survived. Modern carnivores evolved in the form of dogs and cats: 'biting' cats such as those seen today, and 'stabbing' cats or sabre tooths, now extinct.

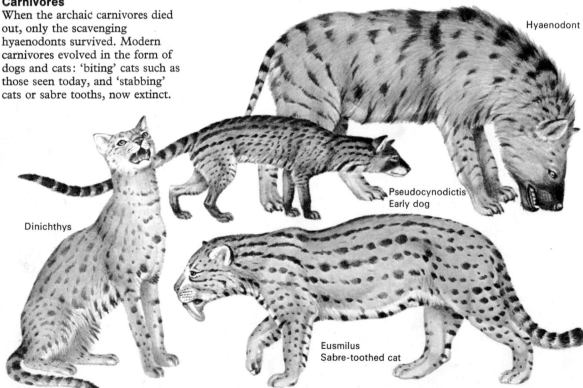

Hyaenodont

Pseudocynodictis
Early dog

Dinichthys

Eusmilus
Sabre-toothed cat

16

The evolution of the horse

Horses developed at the same time as the grasslands started to spread. Because grass is very tough, they needed to develop special grinding teeth; they also needed to be able to escape quickly from predators. Primitive ancestors of the horse had five toes; gradually, these were reduced. A single hoof minimises the likelihood of a sprain when running at speed.

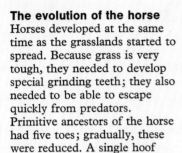

Condylarths were the size of rabbits. Though they retained their stabbing teeth, they also had simple grinding teeth. They had five toes.

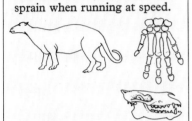

Mesohippus, a primitive horse of 40 million years ago, had only three toes. The canine teeth of its ancestors had disappeared and been replaced by effective grinding teeth.

Equus, the modern horse, has only one toe. Its teeth are very highly crowned and their grinding pattern is very complex. *Equus* can run fast to escape from predators.

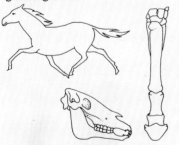

Paraceratherium

Paraceratherium, a hornless rhinoceros of Central Asia, standing six metres high at the shoulder, was the largest land mammal ever.

The grasslands spread

The continuing spread of the grasslands at the expense of the forests had a great effect on animal life during the Miocene period. Life on the open plains gave the herbivores little protection from carnivores. There were few options open to them: one was to grow larger (a carnivore the size of a dog, for instance, is unlikely to attack a herbivore as big as a cow or an elephant); another was to develop weapons, such as horns or tusks, for defence. An added protection was to move about in herds; only the weaker members that could not keep up would then fall victim to the carnivores.

But the easiest solution of all was to become fast runners so that at the approach of danger, they could speed quickly to safety. One advantage of living in open country, however, was the long views: it was not difficult to spot an approaching enemy from a distance, and to take immediate action to avoid it.

The spread of grasslands resulted in the extinction of the cat- and dog-like creodont carnivores. They were quite unable to approach, let alone catch their food, for only animals capable of using their intelligence stood any chance of survival in these conditions.

Modern carnivores descended from the miacids, the cats and dogs,

Life on the open savannah
Many of the mammals that lived on the open savannah during the Miocene period would not be unfamiliar today. The gazelles (1) still look much the same, but the shovel-tusked *Trilophodon* (2) and its elephantine relative, *Deinotherium* (3) would be a strange sight. *Dryopithecus* (4), a small ape-like animal which travelled in troops, and *Moropus* (5), a clawed, horse-like creature, have also been replaced by more advanced forms.

illustrate two different ways of dealing with such a situation. Cats hunt by stealth and cunning, the majority of them on their own. They lie in wait for their victims and then creep stealthily and silently up on them until they are ready to pounce. Dogs on the other hand, hunt in packs, using complicated stratagems to cut off an animal from a herd and then driving it to and fro until its exhaustion allows them to close in for the kill.

Most successful of all mammals in surviving in these new conditions were the descendants of the forest-dwelling *Aegyptopithecus*, the dryopithecines such as *Proconsul*, which spread over the plains of Africa, Asia and Europe. They were small, lightly-built, ape-like creatures which, as individuals, were puny. Without natural weapons of defence, incapable of running away from enemies, they seem to have been the most unlikely inhabitants of open country, with little chance of survival. Yet they flourished and spread over vast areas of the earth. Why? The answer is that with brain power becoming increasingly important, they owed their success to their superior intelligence – as well as to the fact that, like dogs, they moved about in packs, not only for protection but also for hunting.

The shape of man

In the last ten million years, one line of primates has become increasingly dominant: the australopithecines. This form, characterised by the reduction of its sharp, stabbing canine teeth, ousted the lightly-built creatures of the Miocene period.

The success of the australopithecines was aided by their intelligent use of tools. By the start of the Pliocene period, the advanced primates had divided into the more peaceful, gentle apes on the one hand, and the more aggressive group hunters of the human line on the other. Early australopithecines, most of whom were right-handed, hunted with sticks and stones, but as their skills improved, they used bones and teeth as their main source of tools and weapons.

They drove out baboons and other animals from caves so that they could occupy them. They smashed skulls with clubs, even those of their own kind. This type of behaviour was something new in the history of the mammals, heralding the beginning of man's total dominance over the rest of the living world as well as his warlike behaviour towards his fellow man.

There were several different kinds of australopithecines. Some were lightly built; others had massive jaws; a third had a surprisingly large brain. The relationship between these different types is still

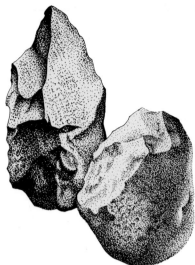

Tools from Olduvai
Many tools have been discovered in East Africa's Olduvai Gorge. Cutting tools and scrapers were made by chipping pebbles together.

20

not generally agreed. Some people believe that the lighter ones were female and the heavier ones male; others argue that they were separate species incapable of interbreeding. It is agreed, however, that they built shelters and advanced from bone to stone tools. Simple though these implements were, it is the organised manufacture of weapons and tools that marks the beginning of mankind.

The fauna, or animal life, of the Pliocene period was similar to that which still inhabits the African plains today. There were antelope, horses, camels, rhinoceroses, hippopotami, elephants, pigs, baboons, and members of the cat and dog families. In addition to these seemingly modern forms, however, there were a number of strange ones, such as the chalicotheres, with their enormous claws and horse-like heads; the deinotheres, which were early elephants and had tusks only on the lower jaw; and *Sivatherium*, a relative of the giraffe which had huge, thick antlers and lived in Asia.

At this time, australopithecines were not yet the undisputed masters of the land; often they fell prey to carnivores, particularly leopards. Predatory animals like australopithecines, cats and dogs, must have fought over the same kills, just as today hyaenas will try to drive a leopard from its kill.

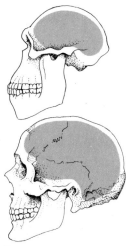

Skulls
Australopithecus had a brain of about 600 cubic centimetres. By comparison, at 1,300 cubic centimetres, the human brain is huge.

Death of a boy
This reconstruction is based on a fossil skull of a boy found with fracture marks made by the stabbing teeth of a leopard. Though *Australopithecus* used tools for weapons, they were not always effective.

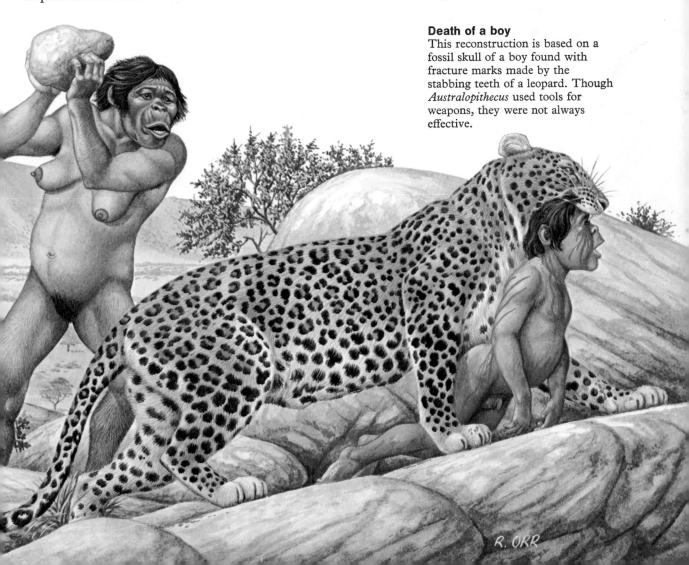

R. ORR

The price of isolation

At the start of the age of mammals, a few primitive forms reached South America from the north, and later, when the two continents separated, they became cut off. The only carnivores were a few marsupials, or pouched mammals, the borhyaenas. In South America, mammals evolved quite independently from the rest of the world, and some unique forms developed. Giant armadillos and ground sloths, for instance, were found only on that continent. But what is most remarkable about South American mammals is the way in which some of them evolved into types which looked exactly like unrelated forms which had developed elsewhere in the world. The proterotheres evolved one-toed 'horses'; the litopterns looked just like llamas; the typotheres developed similarly to rabbits and hares; pyrotheres paralleled elephants; and the toxodonts, which resembled hornless rhinoceroses, developed into both light and heavyweight forms. One marsupial carnivore resembled a sabre-tooth cat:

This evolutionary isolation came to an end when the land bridge across the Panama isthmus was reconnected. Animals familiar today, many of them carnivores, swept down from North America to dominate and overpower those peculiar to South America. The price of earlier isolation was extinction.

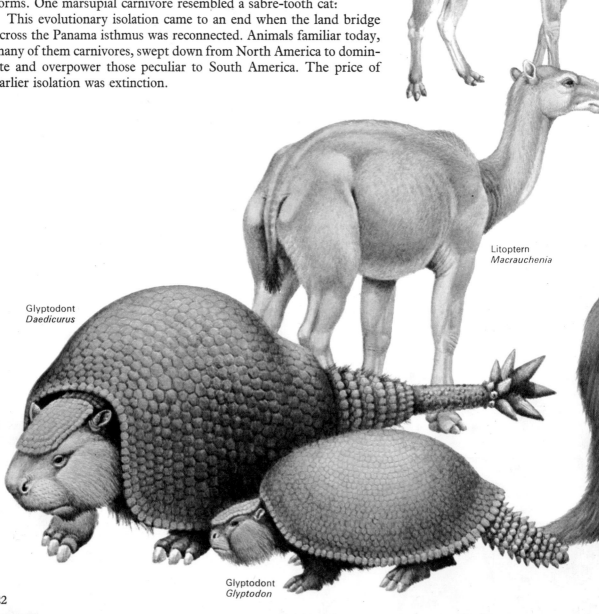

Litoptern
Theosodon

Litoptern
Macrauchenia

Glyptodont
Daedicurus

Glyptodont
Glyptodon

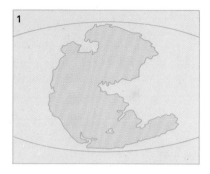

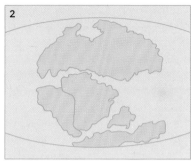

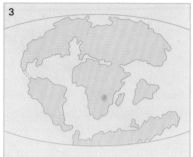

South American mammals

The shape of the continents has not always been the same. 200 million years ago, the world probably contained only one supercontinent, Pangea (1), but about 135 million years ago, Pangea had already begun to split up (2). For a while South America and Africa formed a single continent, while North America remained attached to Europe. Later, South America separated from Africa and began to drift west, and at the same time, North America started to break away from Europe (3). The two continents became linked, only to separate again in the Paleocene period. They rejoined, separated once more, and then eventually adopted the linked position we know today, connected to each other by the Panama isthmus (4).

Giant ground sloth
Megatherium

Proterothere
Thoatherium

Marsupial carnivore
Borhyaena

Marsupial carnivore
Thylacasmilus

Pygmies and giants

The last two million years of the Pleistocene period saw the climax of the age of mammals and, too, its dramatic decline. If seen from a distance, many mammals alive during the earlier part of the Pleistocene would not look unusual today, but closer to, everything would appear magnified. The greater the size, the less risk there was of attack, and this development of giants was taking place all over the world. In North America, some beavers were as big as bears; on the steppes of Asia, the rhinoceros *Elasmotherium* was the size of an elephant; and so, too, were the warthogs in Africa.

Although giants spread across the continents, the reverse process – that of miniaturisation – was taking place on small islands. The animals adapted to the amount of food available to them.

It was the activities of early man that brought to an end the enormous variety of contrasts in size and form once displayed by mammals. Throughout Africa, Asia and Europe, true man, *Homo erectus*, travelled and hunted. Once he had discovered fire and how to control it, he used it both to deter predators and to drive large game animals into traps or over cliffs. The advent of fire was the doom of the large mammals because, by burning the landscape, man destroyed the vegetation that had supported them.

Pygmies
In Malta there were elephants which measured only one metre in height, and even smaller forms of hippo.

Giants

There was no shortage of space on the great continents and during the Pleistocene giant forms of mammals evolved. Some giants, with their modern forms, are seen here.

Giant beaver 2·75 metres long
Modern beaver 1·067 metres long

Giant warthog 3 metres long
Modern warthog 1·5 metres long

Giant hyaena 2·5 metres long
Modern hyaena 1·5 metres long

Giant rhinoceros 6·5 metres long
Modern rhinoceros 3·5 metres long
(Giant rhino horn 2 metres long)

The use of fire

Although man had already learned to use weapons in order to hunt and kill animals, his discovery and control of fire enabled him to dominate everything about him. The animals most vulnerable to this new weapon were the giants; man used fire to destroy the vegetation on which they fed, and as a result many of them became extinct.

The ice ages

During the last million years, the northern continents have been subjected to repeated advances and retreats of ice caps. The mammals that were adapted for life in a cold climate, such as the woolly rhinoceros and hairy mammoth, migrated north when the ice caps retreated, and south when they advanced. The remains of different kinds of mammals found in Europe and North America record this movement of the ice caps.

Man followed the migration of these large game animals. During the last ice age, he recorded many aspects of life at this time in paintings on the sides and roofs of the caves which were his home. Cattle, horses, woolly rhinoceroses and hairy mammoths are all depicted with considerable accuracy.

Although man's camp-sites attracted scavenging and predatory animals, his mastery of fire, and his improved weapons and hunting techniques, meant that he had less to fear. No longer were wolves a serious threat to him; slowly, they became more and more domesticated, feeding on the remains of other animals man had caught. From this point, it is but a short step to the dog continuing his natural hunting role — with the important difference that man was now the leader of the pack.

An ice age scene
During the last ice age, the people of the Ukranian steppes of Russia were completely dependent on the hairy mammoth. In the hunt, the mammoth was man's main quarry, but they also provided him with other benefits. He built houses out of their bones, for example, and covered them with their hides. The remains of one such house that has been discovered show that it was made up of 385 bones from 95 individual mammoths.

The emergence of man

For millions of years, man and his ancestors had been hunters, but of all the mammals, only the dog had become his companion and colleague. About 11,000 years ago, however, a major change in the history of mammals took place, for it was then, in northern Iran, that man first domesticated wild animals – sheep. Instead of hunting them, he herded them. Later, pigs and cattle were also domesticated. So long as they are fed and protected from their natural enemies, these animals are content to be looked after by man. There are human communities today that herd as a way of life, often in difficult and hostile conditions. Herders, like the hunters before them, are nomadic people who travel vast distances with their herds and flocks in search of food. A classic example is the Lapps of northern Europe. The reindeer they herd supply all their basic needs – milk, meat, clothing, and material for making bone tools of all descriptions.

Herders represented the half-way stage between wandering hunters and settled communities. The first permanent human settlements were by rivers and streams, and were fishing villages. The establishment of such villages and their growth, of crop-growing and settled agriculture, and of animal husbandry, all mark the beginnings of human civilisation as we know it today.

The herders
It is easier to herd than to hunt, and when man changed from hunting to herding animals, he started a way of life continued to this day by the Lapps. This idea of herding resulted in owning, and thus conserving, animals.

But the mammals which are now associated with man fall into two basic groups. There are those, such as cats and dogs, that associate with him of their own accord. They have achieved their success because of their intelligence, and are mammals man has always treated sympathetically. The other group of mammals that man has been at pains to care for are those that have provided him with food and clothing. Left to their own devices, they would not choose to associate with him. They are essentially his prey which he has tamed so that when necessary, they can be slaughtered to supply his needs.

Man's pets and his domestic animals are the most established mammals of today, and so long as they continue to prove useful to him, their future is assured. To be exploited by man is a virtual guarantee of survival, for unless mammals can contribute something to his welfare, their future is uncertain and their survival at risk.

Yet there is one further group of mammals connected with man which survives despite man's attempts to exterminate it – the group comprising rats and mice. These rodents have adapted to human civilisation more successfully than any other living creatures. During the last few thousand years, their numbers have increased many times over, and their future survival seems secure.

The farmers
Although he continued to herd, man also began to grow crops and establish settled communities. Some animals became domesticated, but increasing pressure was put on wild animals when man started to take over their habitat for himself.

29

The future of the mammals

The future of the mammals depends on one single species – man. Man is likely to continue to dominate life on this planet for millions of years to come but, as the human population grows, the pressure on the natural resources that sustain wild animals will increase. Whenever it comes to a choice between the needs of man and the needs of other creatures, those of man take precedence because he makes the final decision.

Pigs, sheep, cattle and goats would seem to have an assured future, but the large game animals are doomed unless they are domesticated for food. Man is taking over their habitat and although some may survive for a time in captivity, they will do so only for his education and entertainment.

The age of mammals can be said to have ended with the dominance of one particular mammal – man. The foreseeable future lies with man alone, and only those mammals that can adapt to this situation will survive. There are several ways this can be achieved: to be a friend and companion, the course taken by the most intelligent like cats and dogs; to be a scavenger and pest, that taken by the most agile and cunning; and to be a source of food and other materials needed by man, the option taken by the most docile.

But there is one other alternative, an alternative adopted by mammals during the 140 million years of the age of the dinosaurs: that of keeping out of the way and remaining unnoticed. Ultimately, this is the safest means of ensuring a survival which does not depend on the qualities or success of others. It depends upon a healthy, if uncertain, independence being retained until the dominant form of life quits the stage. Should this happen, should man no longer exist on this planet, then a new age of mammals will certainly dawn.

Dogs and cats
Two animals not endangered by the threat of extinction are dogs and cats. They live under man's dominance and patronage.

Rats and mice
Rats and mice, in spite of man's attempts to exterminate them, flourish today in urban societies. Their survival is one of the rare modern mammal success stories.